The Beatles
Yellow Submarine

A CREATIVE EXPERIENCE

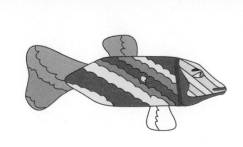

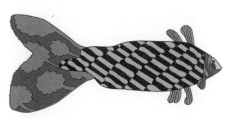
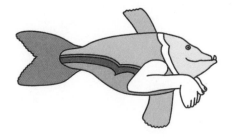

PaRragon

Bath · New York · Cologne · Melbourne · Delhi
Hong Kong · Shenzhen · Singapore

This edition published by Parragon Books Ltd in 2017 and distributed by

Parragon Inc.
440 Park Avenue South, 13th Floor
New York, NY 10016
www.parragon.com

ISBN 978-1-5270-0097-1

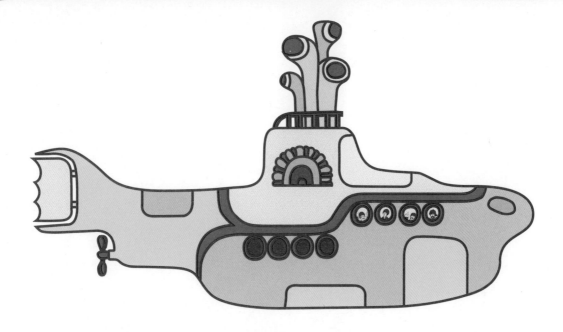

Yellow Submarine

How many words of four or more letters can you make from the words YELLOW SUBMARINE?

To find out how the members of Sgt. Pepper's Lonely Hearts Club Band like to do things, use the code below and fill in the letters.

1	2	3	4	5	6	7	8	9	10	11	12	13	14	15
Z	Y	X	W	V	U	T	S	R	Q	P	O	N	M	L

16	17	18	19	20	21	22	23	24	25	26
K	J	I	H	G	F	E	D	C	B	A

___ ___ ___   ___ ___ ___ ___ ___ ___ ___ ___   ___ ___ ___ !
26 15 15   7 12 20 22 7 19 22 9   13 12 4

Answer on p. 9

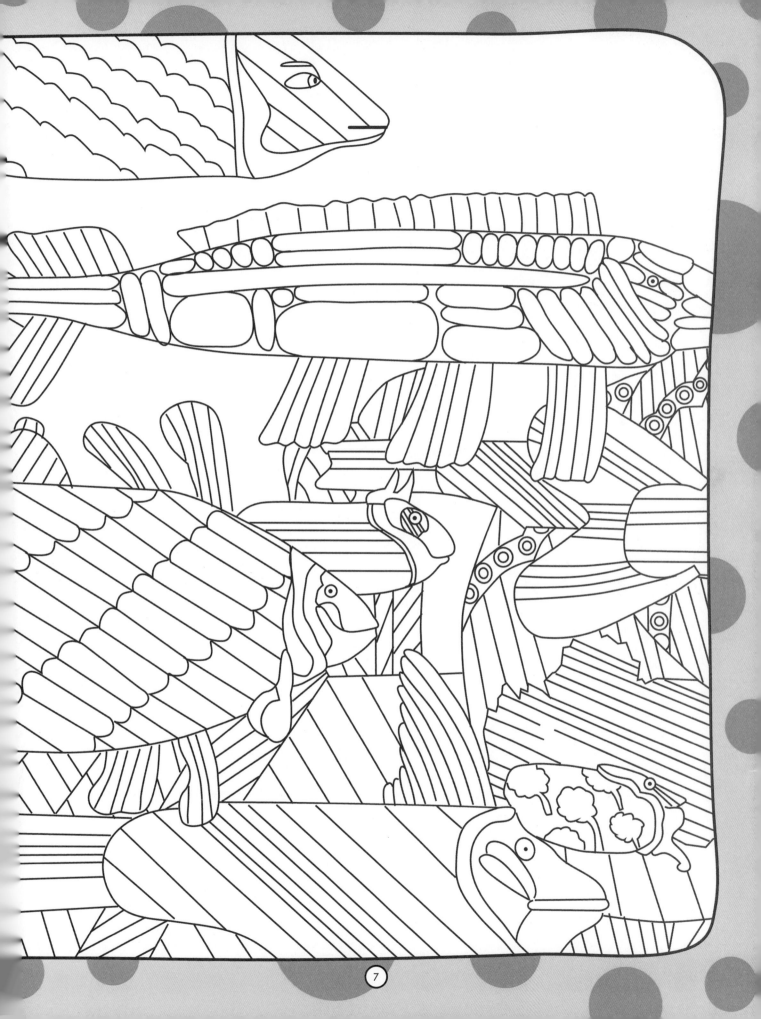

A frantic Fred begs Ringo for HELP, telling him what each letter in the word stands for:

H is for Hurry
E is for Ergent
L is for Love me
P is for P-p-please help

For you, what does each letter of the word HELP stand for?

H _____

E _____

L _____

P _____

Hey Bulldog

There's only one four-headed, blue bulldog, but there are more than 300 breeds of single-headed dogs! How many can you name?

Plants give us the air we breathe; we couldn't live without them. What else couldn't you live without?

See the Seas?

Can you find the following seas from the film in the puzzle?

TIME, SCIENCE, MONSTERS, NOTHING, HOLES, GREEN

Answer on p. 29

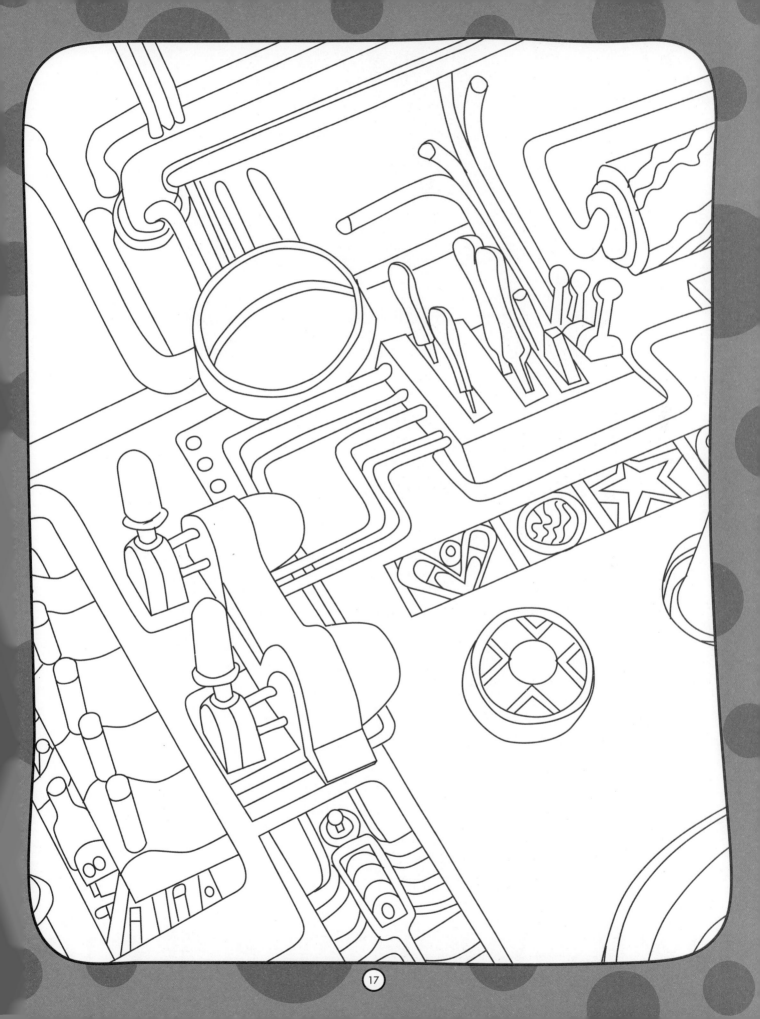

Sixty-four years is **33,638,400** minutes, and one minute is a very long time. What can you draw in one minute?

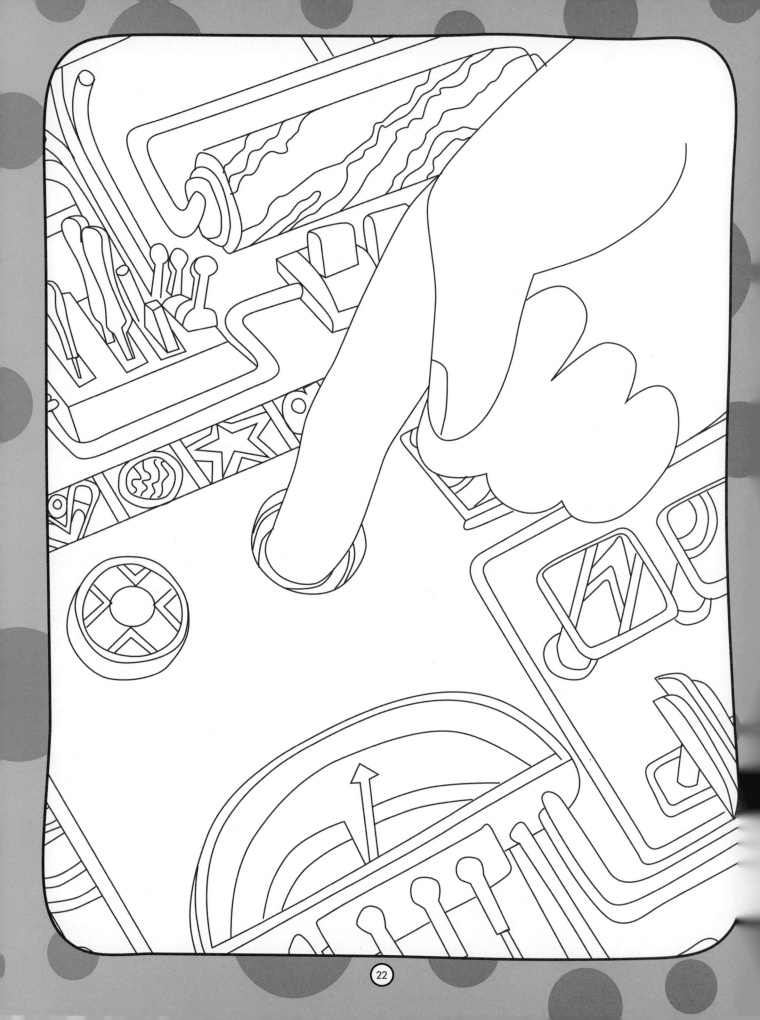

A game for two players. Take turns drawing a horizontal or vertical line between two holes. The goal is to create boxes. The player who completes the fourth side of a box puts their initials inside the box. The game ends when no more lines can be drawn. The player with the most boxes with their initials inside wins the hole thing.

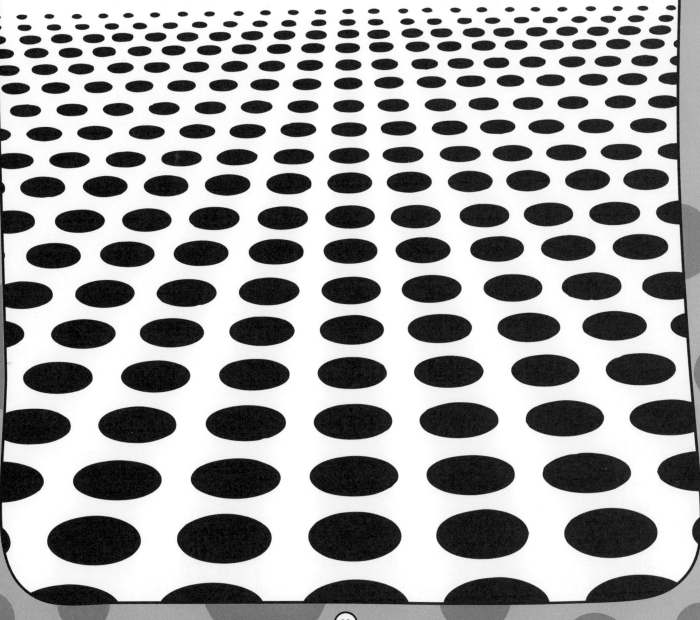

What does love look like to you?

Look, it's a school of whales.

They look a little old for school.

University, then.

How many instruments can you find hidden in the puzzle below?

DRUM, TUBA, TRUMPET, FLUTE, CELLO, VIOLIN, HARP, PIANO, CLARINET, TROMBONE

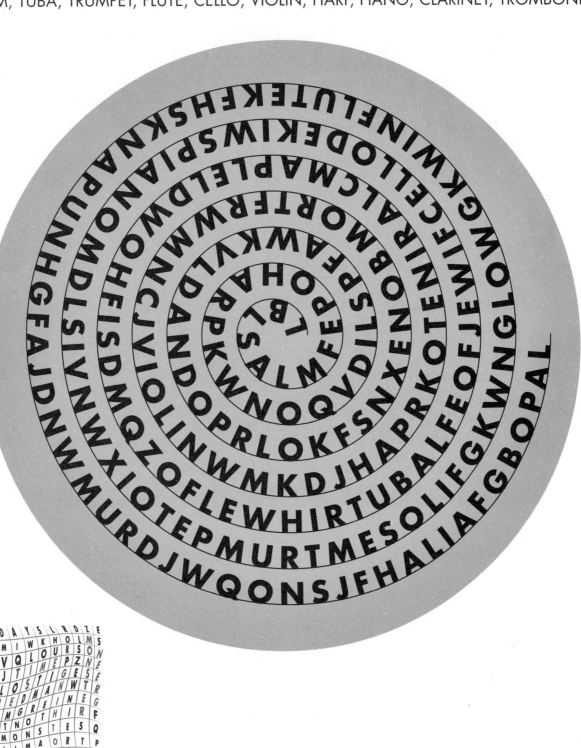

What do you think each of the letters of the word YES stands for?

Y _____

E _____

S _____

Answers from p. 29

What makes you say YES?

I got a hole in me pocket

Seeing double? Not quite.

Find one difference in each pair of images.

Answers on p. 39

Ad hoc, ad loc, and quid pro quo! So little time! So much to know!

What instrument would you play if you were in Sgt. Pepper's Lonely Hearts Club Band? Name a new song you'd write for the band.

Answers for p.33: RINGO: Ring color GEORGE: Cuff color PAUL: Missing pipe JOHN: Wallpaper flower color

What gives you a case of the Blue Meanies?

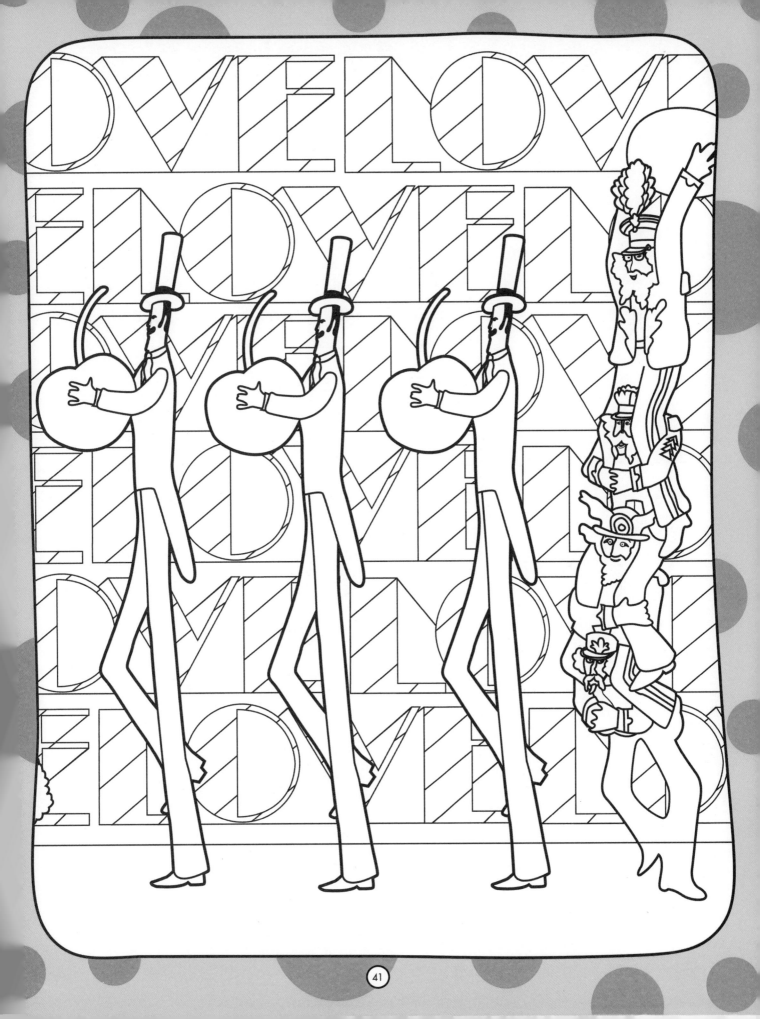

How many times can you find the number 64?

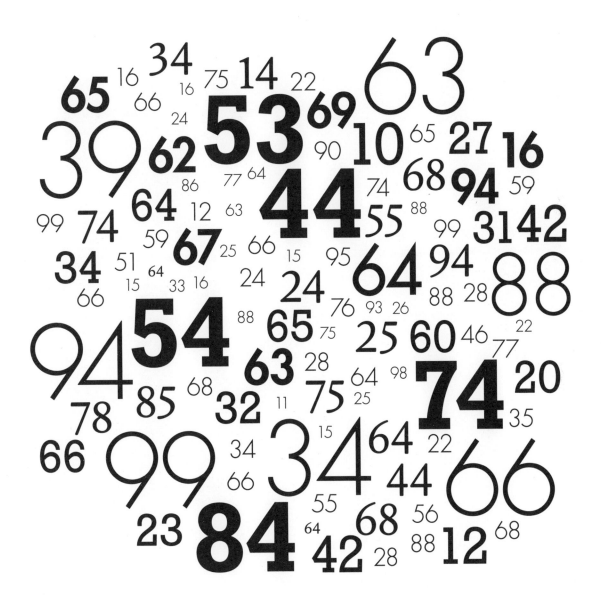

There are plenty of fish in the sea. But there's only one you. What makes you unique?

Draw a creature that belongs in the Sea of Monsters.

Answer for p.46: **7**

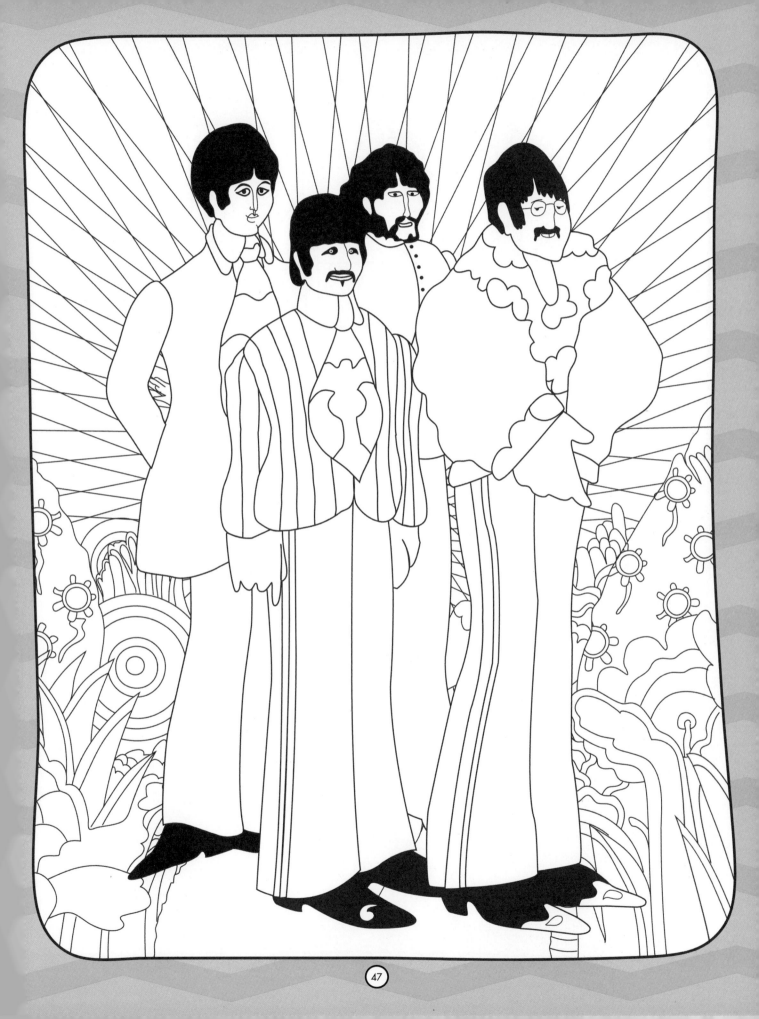

"If I spoke prose, you'd all find out,
I don't know what I talk about."
So says the Nowhere Man.

Could you do worse with verse?
Write a short nonsensical poem.

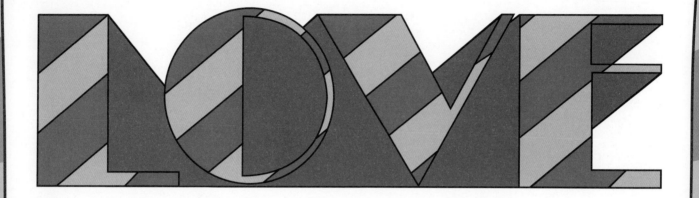

What do each of the letters of the word LOVE stand for to you?

L _____

O _____

V _____

E _____

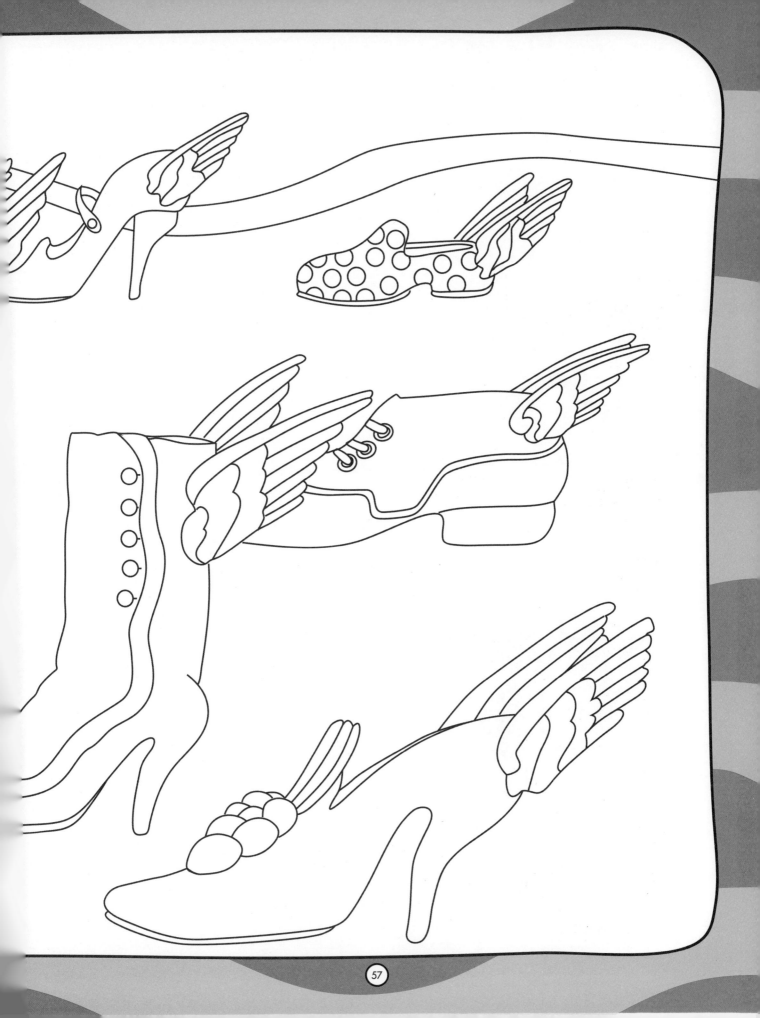

CONGRATULATIONS! You are now an official member of the Sgt. Pepper's Lonely Hearts Club Band. Draw your uniform.

We are all passing through the Sea of Time.
What's on your bucket list?

Color the rainbow in the correct order.

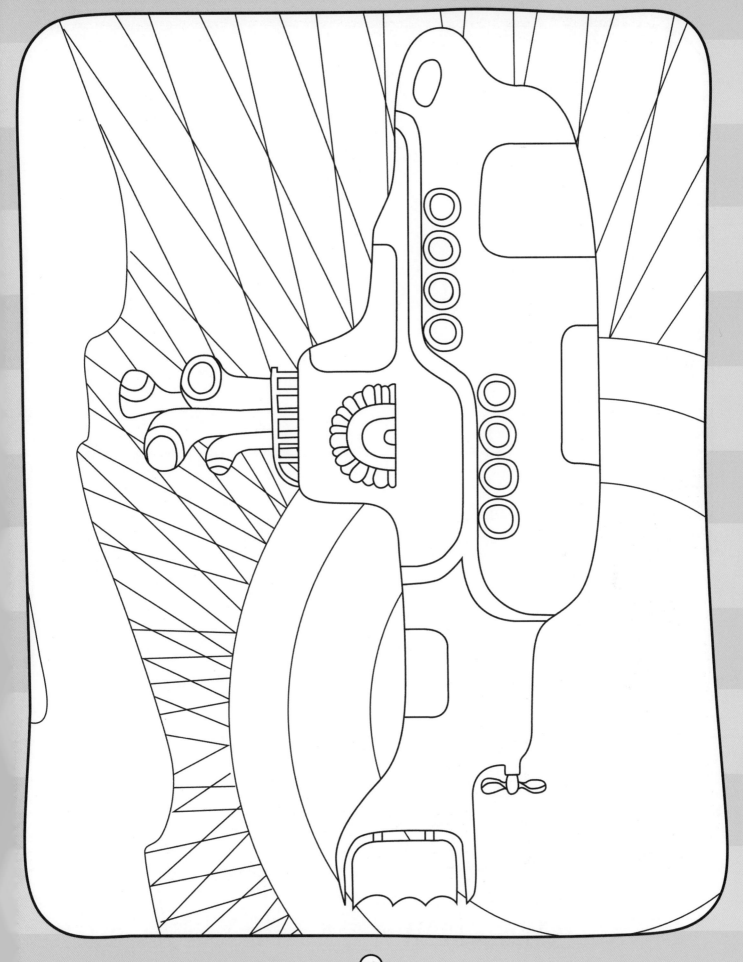